REGENERATIVE AGRRICULTURE

TRANSFORMING FARMING AND OUR PLANET

Linsley Ashley

TABLE OF CONTENT

CHAPTER ONE

The Power of Regenerative Agriculture……………………………..4

CHAPTER TWO

Regenerating Soil Health……………………………………..12

CHAPTER THREE

From Monoculture to Diversity……………………………..20

CHAPTER FOUR

Agroforestry and Silvopasture…………………………………..25

CHAPTER FIVE

Water Management and Conservation…………………………30

CHAPTER SIX

Restoring Ecosystems……………………………………………..35

CHAPTER SEVEN

Regenerative Livestock Management……………………………..41

CHAPTER EIGHT

Regenerative Farming and Social Justice…………………….45

CHAPTER NINE

Regenerative Agriculture and Climate Change……………49

CHAPTER TEN

Regenerative Agriculture in Practice…………………………………..**54**

CHAPTER ELEVEN

Regenerative Agriculture and Policy…………………………………..**60**

CHAPTER TWELVE

Scaling up Regenerative Agriculture………………………………….**64**

CHAPTER THIRTEEN

Regenerating our Future………………………………………………..**68**

CHAPTER ONE

The Power of Regenerative Agriculture

Regenerative agriculture is a holistic agricultural method that emphasizes the interdependence of the health of the soil, the plants, the animals, and the ecosystem. Regenerative agriculture views these elements as interrelated rather than as distinct entities and aims to establish an ecosystem that is self-sustaining and capable of self-regeneration throughout time.

Regenerative agriculture is fundamentally founded on a set of values that give soil health, biodiversity, and ecological resilience first priority. These guidelines consist of:

Enhancing and preserving soil health: Healthy soil is understood to be the cornerstone of regenerative agriculture. Regenerative agriculture can boost plant development, sequester carbon, and enhance soil biology by promoting soil biology, improving soil structure, and increasing soil organic matter.

Crop and livestock diversification: Growing only one type of crop, or monoculture farming, can cause soil degradation, pest outbreaks, and a decline in biodiversity. Regenerative agriculture emphasizes the integration of animals, which can produce organic fertilizer, lessen weed pressure, and enhance soil health. It also promotes a diversity of crops.

Minimizing disturbance: Tillage, or the act of cultivating or plowing the soil, can disturb its organic content, cause erosion, and degrade soil structure. Regenerative farming reduces soil disturbance, allowing for the development of a healthy soil structure by natural processes including root growth and breakdown.

Optimizing animal and plant diversity: Biodiversity is important for the health of ecosystems, and regenerative agriculture places a high priority on protecting and enhancing biodiversity on farms. This can involve growing cover crops, intercropping, and providing wildlife with habitat.

Employing integrated pest management: Regenerative agriculture uses integrated pest management techniques that rely on organic pest control solutions like beneficial insects and companion planting rather than synthetic pesticides and herbicides.

Regenerative farming practices are based on traditional agricultural methods that have been practiced for many years in many regions of the world. These are not new ideas. Yet, the development of industrial agriculture in the 20th century resulted in the widespread use of monoculture farming, artificial inputs, and other methods that are harmful to the biodiversity of the soil and the resilience of the environment. As a result, many agricultural fields have degraded, and farmers are now dealing with more difficult environmental pressures including water scarcity and climate change.

By putting soil health, biodiversity, and ecological resilience first, regenerative agriculture offers a possible response to these problems. Regenerative agriculture can assist farmers in increasing yields, lowering input costs, and developing a more resilient and sustainable food system by helping them build healthy soils, diversify their crops and livestock, minimize soil disturbance, maximize plant and animal diversity, and use integrated pest management.

Regenerative agriculture has the ability to address some of the major environmental issues confronting the world in addition to these on-farm advantages. For instance, strong soils have the capacity to store carbon, lowering greenhouse gas emissions and lessening the effects of climate change. Regenerative agriculture can help pollinators, improve water quality, and improve natural habitats by fostering biodiversity and rebuilding ecosystems. Moreover, regenerative agriculture can aid in lowering waste and minimizing environmental effects by encouraging a more closed-loop system and reducing dependency on synthetic inputs.

A wide range of stakeholders, including farmers, scientists, policymakers, and consumers, are beginning to recognize the potential of regenerative agriculture to improve our food system and heal the planet. Leading organizations in advocating regenerative agricultural practices and assisting farms in switching to these practices include the Rodale Institute, the Savory Institute, and the Regenerative Agriculture Alliance.

Yet, there are still considerable obstacles preventing regenerative agriculture from being widely used. The lack of regenerative practice research and teaching, the high upfront costs of switching to these practices, and the requirement for legislative reforms to support regenerative agriculture at the local, national, and international levels are a few of these. More funding is required for regenerative agriculture research, education, and outreach, as well as for financial incentives and policy changes to aid farmers in switching to these practices.

Notwithstanding these obstacles, regenerative agriculture is now being practiced by many farmers and groups, and the results are encouraging. For instance, by using a mix of cover crops, crop rotations, and no-till techniques, the Gabe Brown farm in North Dakota has been able to increase soil organic matter by 1% per year for the previous 15 years. The Singing Frogs Farm in California uses a system of intensive vegetable production, cover crops, and natural pest management techniques to provide high yields and profitability while requiring little in the way of inputs.

In addition to these case studies of individual achievement, legislators and international organizations are becoming more aware of the potential of regenerative agriculture to address pressing global issues like food security, climate change, and biodiversity loss. For instance, the European Union has incorporated regenerative agriculture into its new Farm to Fork policy and the United Nations Food and Agricultural Organization has identified regenerative agriculture as a critical method for attaining sustainable food systems.

Finally, regenerative agriculture is a potent tool for reshaping our food system and repairing the environment. Regenerative agriculture can assist farmers in increasing yields, lowering input costs, and building a more resilient and sustainable food system by placing a priority on soil health, biodiversity, and ecological resilience. Regenerative agriculture has the ability to address some of the major environmental problems confronting the world today, including as climate change, water scarcity, and biodiversity loss, in addition to these on-farm advantages. Although there are still many obstacles standing in the way of regenerative agriculture's mainstream acceptance, its promise is becoming increasingly recognized, and there are numerous encouraging success stories. Regenerative agriculture has the potential to play a significant role in the development of a more just and sustainable food system for all people, provided that more money is invested in research, education, and policy assistance.

CHAPTER TWO

Regenerating Soil Health

Regenerative agriculture is a comprehensive approach to farming that prioritizes soil, ecosystem, and farmer health. The study of soil health and how to maximize the biological, chemical, and physical qualities of the soil to support plant growth and ecosystem resilience are at the heart of regenerative agriculture. In this essay, we will delve into the science of regenerative agriculture and investigate how it might improve soil health, increase biodiversity, and store carbon.

The Soil Health Science

Soil health is a complex and dynamic system influenced by biological, chemical, and physical elements. Soil is, at its most basic, a mixture of minerals, organic materials, water, and air. The complex web of interactions between microbes, plants, and nutrients that occurs within the soil, on the other hand, is what makes soil healthy.

The relevance of soil organic matter is an important notion in regenerative agriculture. Soil organic matter is the result of soil microbes decomposing plant and animal debris. It is an important source of nutrients for plants and is necessary for the development of a healthy soil structure and water-holding capacity. Soil organic matter is especially important in carbon sequestration since it stores carbon in a stable form for decades to centuries.

Soil structure is another essential aspect in soil health. The arrangement of soil particles and the spaces between them are referred to as soil structure. A healthy soil structure is essential for water infiltration, root growth, and air exchange. A variety of factors influence soil structure, including soil texture, organic matter content, and soil biology.

Soil biology is an important component of soil health since it is involved in nutrient cycling, carbon sequestration, and plant growth. Bacteria, fungus, protozoa, and nematodes are examples of soil microorganisms. These microbes create symbiotic connections with plant roots, which are essential for plant growth and health. Mycorrhizal fungi, for example, create connections with plant roots to help plants get nutrients such as phosphorus and nitrogen. Soil microbes are also important in the breakdown of organic materials and the release of nutrients for plant uptake.

Soil Health and Regenerative Agriculture

Regenerative agriculture is a comprehensive farming method that emphasizes soil health, biodiversity, and ecosystem resilience. Regenerative agriculture encompasses a variety of strategies aimed at improving soil health and supporting a diversified and resilient ecosystem. Some of the most important practices in regenerative agriculture are:

Cover crops are plants that are grown to cover the soil in between cash crops. Cover crops can help to improve soil structure, minimize erosion, and increase soil organic matter. Cover crops can also aid in weed control and provide habitat for beneficial insects.

Reduced tillage: Tillage refers to mechanical soil manipulation. Reduced tillage measures, such as no-till or conservation tillage, can aid in the preservation of soil structure, the reduction of erosion, and the promotion of soil biology. Tillage reduction can also help to minimize carbon emissions by lowering fuel usage and soil disturbance.

Crop rotation is the process of alternating the crops planted in a specific land over time. Crop rotation can aid in the breakup of disease cycles, the improvement of soil fertility, and the reduction of weed pressure. Crop rotation can also aid in ecosystem diversification by providing habitat for a variety of useful creatures.

Agroforestry is the practice of incorporating trees into agricultural settings. Agroforestry can assist enhance soil health, trap carbon, and provide wildlife habitat. Agroforestry can also give farmers with extra income streams by producing lumber, fruits, or nuts.

Integrating livestock: Grazing animals are integrated into cropping systems as part of livestock integration. Cattle integration can help to improve nitrogen cycling, increase soil organic matter, and reduce the requirement for synthetic fertilizers. Grazing animals can also help farmers manage weeds and pests while also providing alternative income streams through the production of meat, milk, or wool.

These regenerative methods are founded on agro ecological concepts, which are a science-based approach to agriculture that promotes the incorporation of ecological principles and social values into farming systems. Agriculture is recognized as a complex system influenced by a variety of biological, social, and environmental elements, and agricultural systems must be planned to optimize these interactions in an ecologically and socially sustainable manner.

Regenerative Agriculture's Potential

Regenerative agriculture has the ability to completely revolutionize our food system while also healing the earth. Regenerative agriculture can aid by addressing soil health, biodiversity, and ecosystem resilience.

Increase soil health: Regenerative agriculture approaches can help to increase soil organic matter, structure, and biology. This can result in increased soil fertility, water retention capacity, and nutrient availability, which can boost plant growth and productivity.

Enhance biodiversity: Regenerative agricultural approaches can aid in the development of diverse and resilient ecosystems that support a diverse spectrum of plant and animal life. This can aid in the promotion of pollination, pest management, and other ecosystem services vital to agricultural output.

Carbon sequestration: Regenerative agriculture practices can aid in the sequestration of carbon in soil organic matter, which can aid in the mitigation of climate change. Regenerative agricultural approaches have been demonstrated in studies to absorb considerable amounts of carbon, which can assist to offset greenhouse gas emissions from the agriculture industry.

Increase resilience: Regenerative agriculture approaches can aid in the development of resilient farming systems capable of dealing with climate change, pests, and other environmental challenges. Regenerative agriculture can help to produce more resilient and adaptive farming systems by diversifying cropping systems and encouraging ecosystem services.

Support rural communities: Regenerative agriculture practices can aid in the development of more diversified and resilient rural economies, which can aid in the support of local communities and the reduction of poverty.

Conclusion

Regenerative agriculture is a science-based agricultural method that emphasizes soil health, biodiversity, and ecosystem resilience. Farmers may improve soil health, increase biodiversity, store carbon, and develop more resilient and adaptive farming systems by employing a variety of regenerative strategies. Regenerative agriculture has the potential to alter our food system and heal the planet, all while benefiting local communities and encouraging social and economic sustainability.

CHAPTER THREE

From Monoculture to Diversity

For many years, the agricultural business relied primarily on monoculture practices, which entail producing a single crop species across a broad amount of land. While this strategy can result in high yields in the near term, it has also been linked to a number of environmental and socioeconomic issues, including soil erosion, nutrient depletion, and biodiversity loss. There has been a surge of interest in regenerative agriculture in recent years, which advocates crop diversification as a fundamental method for increasing soil health, reducing reliance on synthetic inputs, and building a more resilient and sustainable food system.

Crop Diversity Is Critical

Crop diversity refers to the number of crop species, types, and genetic features grown in an agricultural system. A diversified farming system can give several advantages, including:

Soil health can be improved by diversifying cropping systems by increasing soil organic matter, minimizing erosion, and promoting nutrient cycling. This can result in higher soil fertility, water retention capacity, and resistance to environmental pressures.

Reduced pest and disease pressure: Diversified cropping systems can help to minimize pest and disease pressure by decreasing pest and disease buildup in certain crops. Farmers can build a more complex and diversified environment that is less susceptible to pest and disease outbreaks by rotating crops and intercropping.

Improved resilience: By establishing a more resilient and adaptive farming system, diverse cropping patterns can help to increase resilience. Farmers can construct a system that is better equipped to cope with environmental pressures such as drought, floods, and severe temperatures by producing a variety of crops with varied characteristics.

Diversified cropping systems can help to increase food security by lowering the chance of crop failure and increasing the availability of a variety of food crops. This can aid in providing communities with a broad and nutritious diet.

Crop Diversity through Regenerative Agriculture Practices

Crop diversity is promoted through a variety of regenerative agriculture approaches, including:

Crop rotation is the practice of producing different crops in a series or rotation throughout time. This can aid in the improvement of soil health, the reduction of insect and disease pressure, and the growth of yields.

Intercropping is the practice of planting multiple crops on the same field. This can contribute to the development of a more diversified and complex ecosystem that is less susceptible to pest and disease outbreaks.

Planting a non-cash crop, such as a legume or grass, in between cash crops is known as cover cropping. This can aid in improving soil health, reducing erosion, and increasing nutrient cycling.

The practice of integrating trees into farming systems is known as agroforestry. This can assist to improve soil health, sequester carbon, and offer farmers with extra income sources.

Crop Diversity's Advantages in Regenerative Agriculture

Crop diversification is promoted as a fundamental method for increasing soil health, reducing reliance on synthetic inputs, and building a more resilient and sustainable food system. Farmers may construct diversified and robust farming systems that are better equipped to cope with environmental challenges while also supporting local communities and promoting social and economic sustainability by employing a variety of regenerative methods.

Finally, regenerative agriculture provides a promising approach for transforming our agricultural systems from monoculture to diversity. Regenerative agriculture can help to improve soil health, reduce pest and disease pressure, build resilience, and improve food security by promoting crop diversity. As such, it is a potent weapon for establishing a more sustainable and equitable food system for all.

CHAPTER FOUR

Agroforestry and Silvopasture

Two cutting-edge farming techniques that entail incorporating trees into agricultural systems are agroforestry and silvopasture. Recent years have seen an upsurge in interest in these techniques due to their capacity to boost biodiversity, soil health, and carbon sequestration.

In agroforestry, trees or bushes are grown alongside or in close proximity to pastureland or crops. Agroforestry technique known as silvopasture combines pastureland for animal grazing with trees. These methods have a number of advantages that can enhance climate change mitigation and sustainable agriculture.

Enhancing Soil Health

By boosting nutrient cycling, decreasing erosion, and increasing organic matter, integrating trees into farming systems can assist to improve soil health. Via their branches, leaves, and falling leaves, trees can serve as a supply of organic matter. These organic materials can enhance soil fertility, structure, and water-holding capacity.

By stabilizing slopes and lowering runoff, trees can also aid in decreasing soil erosion. Deep soil penetration by tree roots can also aid to improve soil structure and avoid compaction.

Increasing Biodiversity

By building a more intricate and varied ecology, agroforestry and silvopasture can aid in improving biodiversity. A variety of animals, such as birds, mammals, and insects, can find habitat in trees. Moreover, a variety of plants, including species that can tolerate shade, can thrive in the understory of trees.

A more resilient farming system that is better equipped to withstand environmental pressures like drought and pests can be created thanks to the enhanced biodiversity that comes from agroforestry and silvopasture.

More Carbon Sequestration

As a result of photosynthesis, trees are renowned for their capacity to capture carbon dioxide from the atmosphere. Agroforestry and silvopasture can help to enhance the amount of carbon that is stored in the soil and in the trees themselves by incorporating trees into farming systems.

Agroforestry and silvopasture can aid in lowering greenhouse gas emissions in addition to sequestering carbon. These procedures can lessen the demand for artificial fertilizers and other inputs, which can assist to lessen agriculture's carbon footprint.

Additional Advantages

Agroforestry and silvopasture can offer farmers and the surrounding area benefits in addition to those mentioned above. For instance, trees can give livestock shade, lowering heat stress and enhancing animal wellbeing. By the sale of lumber, fruits, nuts, and other tree products, they can also offer farmers extra sources of revenue.

Challenges and Things to Think About

While agroforestry and silvopasture have many advantages, there are some drawbacks and things to bear in mind as well. For instance, including trees into farming systems may necessitate additional management and planning, as well as possible land-use trade-offs.

Also, the design of the agroforestry or silvopasture system and the choice of tree species can have a big impact on how well it works. In order to prevent conflict with crops or grazing, it is crucial to choose tree species that are suitable for the area's climate and soil conditions. Careful planning should also go into the spacing and arrangement of the trees.

Conclusion

Agroforestry and silvopasture are two cutting-edge farming techniques that provide a number of advantages for increased biodiversity, soil health, and carbon sequestration. These methods are a crucial tool for advancing sustainable farming and reducing the effects of climate change.

Agroforestry and silvopasture systems can present certain difficulties and obstacles, but because of the advantages they provide, they are an important tool in the regenerative agriculture toolbox.

CHAPTER FIVE

Water Management and Conservation

Water is a valuable resource that is required for agricultural productivity. Water scarcity and drought are becoming more widespread as the effects of climate change worsen, making water management and conservation a critical problem for farmers worldwide. Regenerative agriculture approaches provide a variety of solutions for water conservation, drought mitigation, and mitigating the effects of climate change on agriculture.

Water Conservation Via Soil Health

Improving soil health is one of the most important ways that regenerative agricultural practices can assist to preserve water. Healthy soils can absorb and retain more water, lowering runoff and boosting water-holding capacity. This implies that crops may get the water they need more easily, especially during droughts.

Cover cropping, decreased tillage, and crop rotation can help to improve soil health by increasing organic matter, improving soil structure, and enhancing nutrient cycling. These methods can also help to prevent soil erosion, as well as water loss and soil moisture.

Water Conservation and Irrigation Efficiency

Regenerative agriculture approaches can help to conserve water by improving water harvesting and irrigation efficiency, in addition to improving soil health. Water harvesting techniques such as swales, berms, and contour farming can assist in capturing and storing rainwater, lowering the need for irrigation and conserving water.

Drip irrigation and micro-sprinklers, for example, can help to minimize water use by delivering water directly to plant roots, reducing runoff and evaporation. These systems can be paired with soil moisture monitoring techniques to guarantee that crops receive the appropriate amount of water at the appropriate time, decreasing water waste even further.

Drought Reduction

By strengthening the resilience of farming systems, regenerative agriculture approaches can also help to alleviate the effects of drought. Regenerative agricultural strategies can help crops withstand droughts and prevent crop failure by improving soil health and conserving water.

Furthermore, measures like cover cropping and crop rotation can help diversify farming systems, reducing reliance on a particular crop and making them more adaptable to the effects of climate change. Trees can also be included into farming systems to provide shade and prevent soil moisture loss, so boosting the system's resilience.

Minimizing Climate Change's Effects on Agriculture

Climate change is having a substantial impact on agriculture, making farming more difficult due to rising temperatures, shifting precipitation patterns, and more frequent extreme weather events. Regenerative agricultural approaches provide a variety of options for mitigating the effects of climate change on agriculture.

Regenerative agriculture strategies can help crops better tolerate the effects of climate change by improving soil health and conserving water, lowering the risk of crop failure and increasing yields. Furthermore, cover crops and crop rotation can assist to trap carbon in the soil, lowering greenhouse gas emissions and minimizing the effects of climate change.

Considerations and Obstacles

While regenerative agriculture approaches provide a variety of solutions for water conservation and lessening the effects of climate change, there are some obstacles and issues to be aware of. Implementing water harvesting and irrigation systems, for example, can necessitate significant upfront expenditure as well as additional monitoring and planning.

Furthermore, crop selection and farming system design can have a substantial impact on success. To avoid water competition, it is critical to select crops that are appropriate for the local temperature and soil conditions, as well as carefully arrange the layout of the farming system.

Conclusion

Water conservation and management are crucial challenges for farmers all over the world. Regenerative agriculture approaches provide a variety of solutions for water conservation, drought mitigation, and mitigating the effects of climate change on agriculture. Regenerative agricultural approaches improve soil health, increase water harvesting and irrigation efficiency, and diversify farming systems.

CHAPTER SIX

Restoring Ecosystems

Human activities such as deforestation, agriculture, and urbanization have had substantial affects on ecosystems and the services they provide, making ecosystem degradation a growing concern around the world. Regenerative agriculture approaches provide a variety of solutions for rebuilding degraded ecosystems and sustaining ecosystem services like pollination, insect control, and nutrient cycling.

Agroforestry for Ecosystem Restoration

Agroforestry is one of the most important ways that regenerative agriculture methods can aid in ecosystem restoration. Agroforestry is the practice of incorporating trees into farming systems, and it can provide numerous benefits to both agriculture and ecosystems.

Agroforestry trees can shade crops, lowering the demand for irrigation and boosting soil moisture. They can also aid to prevent soil erosion and provide wildlife habitat, so promoting biodiversity and ecosystem function.

Furthermore, trees can provide a variety of ecosystem services vital to agricultural output, such as pollination and pest control. Bees and other pollinators, for example, are critical to the pollination of many crops, and trees can provide vital habitat for these species.

Crop Variety Increases Biodiversity

Crop diversity is another way that regenerative agriculture practices can help with ecosystem restoration. Monoculture farming methods, in which a single crop is farmed over a broad region, can harm biodiversity and ecosystem function.

Crop rotation and intercropping are two regenerative agricultural strategies that can assist enhance crop diversity, reduce reliance on a single crop, and improve ecosystem function. These practices can sustain biodiversity and improve ecosystem resilience by providing various habitats and food sources for wildlife.

Nutritional Cycling Support

Regenerative agriculture approaches can also help to preserve soil health and agricultural output by promoting nutrient cycling in ecosystems. The process through which nutrients are taken up by plants, recycled through the soil, and made accessible for use by other species is referred to as nutrient cycling.

Cover cropping, crop rotation, and reduced tillage can all serve to support nutrient cycling by increasing organic matter in the soil and improving nutrient availability. These techniques can assist to reduce the demand for synthetic fertilizers while also promoting soil health by promoting the natural cycle of nutrients through the soil.

Integrated Pest Management and Pest Control

By the application of integrated pest management, regenerative agriculture approaches can also aid in pest control in ecosystems (IPM). IPM is a holistic pest control technique that tries to reduce the usage of synthetic pesticides while promoting natural pest control approaches.

Crop rotation, intercropping, and the use of cover crops are regenerative agricultural strategies that can help to reduce pest populations by disturbing pest habitat and food supplies. Furthermore, the utilization of natural predators such as birds and insects can aid in pest population management without the usage of synthetic pesticides.

Considerations and Obstacles

While regenerative agriculture approaches provide a variety of solutions for repairing ecosystems and providing ecosystem services, they also provide significant obstacles and issues. Implementing agroforestry systems, for example, can necessitate significant upfront investment as well as additional maintenance and planning.

Furthermore, crop selection and farming system design can have a substantial impact on success. To sustain biodiversity and ecosystem function, it is critical to select crops that are suited for the local temperature and soil conditions, as well as carefully arrange the structure of the agricultural system.

Conclusion

Repairing degraded ecosystems and providing ecosystem services is crucial for agricultural sustainability and the health of our planet in the long run. Regenerative agricultural approaches provide a variety of solutions for ecosystem restoration, biodiversity enhancement, natural nutrient cycling, and insect management. Regenerative agriculture strategies can help to restore ecosystems and support services by incorporating trees into farming systems, boosting crop diversity, and supporting natural pest control methods.

CHAPTER SEVEN

Regenerative Livestock Management

Crop cultivation is only one aspect of regenerative agriculture. Cattle management is another crucial aspect of regenerative agriculture. We will look at the ideas and benefits of regenerative livestock management in this chapter.

Traditional livestock management practices, such as confined animal feeding operations (CAFOs), have harmed the environment by causing soil erosion and water contamination. Regenerative livestock management, on the other hand, seeks to improve soil health, promote biodiversity, and reduce greenhouse gas emissions while also enhancing animal wellbeing.

Rotational grazing is a major element of regenerative livestock management. This is shifting livestock from one pasture to another in order to give the plants time to rest and recover. This contributes to soil health by helping the soil to absorb more water, store more minerals, and encourage healthy microbial activity.

In addition to rotational grazing, regenerative livestock management includes mixed-species grazing, which involves grazing different species of animals together, and regenerative grazing, which involves managing cattle in a way that reflects natural grazing patterns. This promotes biodiversity and improves soil health.

Regenerative livestock management has the potential to lower greenhouse gas emissions. Livestock that is maintained in a regenerative manner helps to sequester carbon in the soil. This is due to the fact that healthy soil has more organic matter, which is composed of carbon. Furthermore, regenerative grazing practices can reduce the requirement for synthetic fertilizers, which contribute significantly to greenhouse gas emissions.

Regenerative livestock management can boost animal welfare in addition to environmental benefits. Regenerative livestock management can minimize stress on livestock and enhance their general health by giving access to pasture and supporting natural grazing patterns.

Holistic planned grazing is one type of regenerative livestock management. This entails organizing livestock movements depending on the individual demands of the land, the animals, and the environment. Holistic planned grazing can improve soil health, boost biodiversity, and increase productivity by carefully controlling grazing patterns.

Silvopasture, which involves incorporating trees into livestock pasture systems, is another example of regenerative livestock management. This provides shade for the animals, which can increase their welfare while also lowering heat stress and water consumption. Trees also store carbon, promote soil health, and give wildlife habitat.

Regenerative livestock management entails decreasing the use of synthetic inputs such as antibiotics and hormones, in addition to these specific approaches. Instead, cattle are handled in such a way that their natural health and immunity are enhanced.

Ultimately, regenerative livestock management has the potential to change the livestock business by lowering greenhouse gas emissions, improving soil health, and increasing biodiversity. Regenerative livestock management can help establish a more sustainable and resilient food system by increasing natural grazing patterns, decreasing synthetic inputs, and integrating livestock into healthy ecosystems.

CHAPTER EIGHT

Regenerative Farming and Social Justice

Regenerative agriculture is concerned with not only environmental but also social sustainability. It has the potential to build a more just and equitable food system for farmers, farmworkers, and communities. We will look at the social and economic benefits of regenerative agriculture, as well as how it may promote food sovereignty and fairness.

One of the primary advantages of regenerative agriculture is the potential for economic opportunities for small farmers and communities. Crop diversification and agroforestry, for example, can boost yields and improve soil health, resulting in improved income for farmers. This can aid in the development of more resilient and self-sufficient communities.

Regenerative agriculture can also provide farmworkers with economic prospects. Regenerative agriculture, by fostering more diverse and sustainable farming practices, can provide more stable and secure employment possibilities for farmworkers, who are frequently subjected to exploitative labor practices in conventional agriculture.

Another advantage of regenerative agriculture is that it might help to increase food sovereignty. Food sovereignty refers to people's right to healthy, culturally acceptable food produced using environmentally sound and sustainable techniques, as well as their right to define their own food and agriculture systems. By allowing communities to produce their own food using sustainable and culturally relevant ways, regenerative agriculture can assist to foster food sovereignty.

Regenerative agriculture can promote equity in addition to food sovereignty. Regenerative agriculture can assist to minimize economic inequality in rural regions by generating economic opportunities for small farmers and farmworkers. It can also promote social justice by improving access to healthful, culturally appropriate meals.

By preserving traditional farming practices and supporting indigenous knowledge systems, regenerative agriculture can also promote social and cultural sustainability. Several indigenous cultures have long practiced regenerative agriculture, and regenerative agriculture can assist to maintain cultural legacy and encourage intergenerational knowledge transmission by supporting these practices.

There are, however, obstacles to fostering social justice and equity through regenerative agriculture. One difficulty is that regenerative agriculture approaches can be resource-intensive and expensive. This can make it difficult for small farmers and towns with little resources to enter the market.

There is also a need to address power imbalances within the food chain. Many farmers and farmworkers are exploited, and the concentration of power in the hands of a few large agribusinesses can limit chances for small farmers and communities.

To solve these issues, it is critical to push policies that encourage regenerative agriculture as well as fairness and social justice. Policies that provide financing and technical aid to small farmers and communities, as well as policies that encourage worker protections and farmworker rights, are examples of this.

Finally, regenerative agriculture has the potential to build a more just and equitable food system that benefits farmers, farmworkers, and communities. Regenerative agriculture can help to develop more resilient and self-sufficient communities that are better able to face the issues of environmental degradation and climate change by encouraging food sovereignty, equity, and social and cultural sustainability.

CHAPTER NINE

Regenerative Agriculture and Climate Change

One of the most urgent problems facing humanity today is climate change. Rising temperatures, extreme weather events, sea level rise, and other effects are already having an impact on ecosystems and human communities. Agriculture is both a cause and a result of climate change. Regenerative agriculture, on the other hand, has the potential to reduce greenhouse gas emissions, increase carbon sequestration, and improve resistance to the effects of climate change.

Reducing greenhouse gas emissions is one of the key ways that regenerative agriculture can help to reduce climate change. Agriculture accounts for around 13% of global greenhouse gas emissions, making conventional agriculture a significant contributor to greenhouse gas emissions. Regenerative agricultural strategies, such as reduced tillage, cover crops, and livestock integration, can reduce greenhouse gas emissions by improving soil health and decreasing the demand for synthetic fertilizers and pesticides.

Regenerative agriculture can trap carbon in soil and vegetation as well as reduce greenhouse gas emissions. Soil is a large carbon sink, and regenerative agriculture strategies such as cover cropping, agroforestry, and rotational grazing can improve soil carbon storage. Regenerative agriculture can assist to offset greenhouse gas emissions and mitigate the effects of climate change by sequestering carbon in the soil and vegetation.

Regenerative agriculture can also help to mitigate climate change by lowering emissions connected with food transportation. Regenerative agriculture encourages local and regional food systems, which can shorten the distance between farm and table. This can help to minimize transportation-related emissions while also supporting local economies.

Regenerative agriculture can also help with climate change adaption by strengthening farming systems.

Climate change is anticipated to increase the frequency and intensity of extreme weather events including droughts, floods, and storms, which can have disastrous consequences for agriculture. Regenerative agricultural strategies, such as water management, agroforestry, and crop diversification, on the other hand, can serve to improve farming system resilience and mitigate the effects of extreme weather events.

Water management strategies are one example of how regenerative agriculture can boost resilience. Water collection and conservation measures, for example, can help to minimize the effects of drought by improving crop water availability. Similarly, agroforestry activities like planting trees along waterways can help to mitigate the effects of flooding by boosting soil's ability to absorb and hold water.

In addition to mitigating the effects of extreme weather events, regenerative agriculture can improve soil health and biodiversity, hence increasing the resilience of farming systems. Soils that are healthy and diversified are better equipped to tolerate the effects of climate change, such as pest and disease outbreaks.

Yet, promoting regenerative agriculture as a climate change mitigation and adaptation method is fraught with difficulties. One difficulty is that regenerative agriculture approaches can be expensive and may not be appropriate for all farming systems. Furthermore, legislative and market hurdles to the implementation of regenerative agriculture approaches must be addressed.

To solve these difficulties, regulations and market incentives that favor regenerative agriculture techniques must be promoted. These can include regulations that offer farmers with cash and technical assistance, as well as market incentives for practicing sustainable agriculture. It is also critical to enhance education and outreach in order to improve awareness and stimulate adoption of regenerative agriculture.

Finally, regenerative agriculture has the ability to prevent and adapt to the effects of climate change by lowering greenhouse gas emissions, boosting carbon sequestration, and strengthening farming systems' resilience. We can support a more sustainable and resilient food system that benefits both people and the earth by encouraging regenerative agriculture methods and removing policy and market impediments.

CHAPTER TEN

Regenerative Agriculture in Practice

On farms and ranches all across the world, regenerative agriculture is being practiced rather than merely being a theoretical idea. We will examine some actual instances of regenerative agriculture in this chapter and gain insight from farmers and organizations that have adopted this method of farming.

A modest family farm in northern California called Singing Frogs Farm is one such instance. Paul and Elizabeth Kaiser, who have been using regenerative agriculture for more than ten years, are the farm's owners and operators. In spite of its tiny size and lack of mechanization, Singing Frogs Farm is renowned for its high yields and profitability. The Kaisers credit their success to the adoption of regenerative techniques like composting, crop rotation, cover crops, and no-till farming. They have developed a robust ecosystem that supports a variety of crops and helpful insects by imitating the natural processes of soil formation and nutrient cycling.

The work of the Savory Institute, a global network of farmers, ranchers, and scientists who are advocating regenerative grazing practices, is another illustration of regenerative agriculture in action. Allan Savory, a rancher and biologist from Zimbabwe who created the holistic management paradigm for land management, founded the Savory Institute. Holistic management is carefully controlling grazing livestock to resemble the typical foraging behaviors of wild herbivores. Thus doing can enhance water infiltration and retention, sequester carbon, and assist recover degraded grasslands. The Savory Institute collaborates with farmers and ranchers all around the world to implement regenerative grazing techniques and other forms of holistic management.

The Rodale Institute, a non-profit research organization devoted to studying and promoting organic farming and regenerative agriculture, provides a third illustration of regenerative agriculture in action. Since it began studying regenerative agriculture more than 70 years ago, the Rodale Institute has shown the advantages of techniques like crop rotation, cover crops, and decreased tillage for enhancing soil health, locking up carbon, and boosting yields. The Rodale Institute also runs a 333-acre research farm in Pennsylvania where they carry out research and show how regenerative agriculture is used in real-world situations.

These are just a handful of the several farmers and groups who are adopting regenerative agriculture and showcasing how it has the power to improve our food system and heal the earth. We may anticipate that regenerative agriculture will continue to gather momentum and spread as more and more people become aware of its advantages. Regenerative agriculture presents a possible future route because of its emphasis on improving biodiversity, conserving water, reducing climate change, and restoring soil health.

There are other larger movements and efforts that aim to promote regenerative agriculture on a larger scale in addition to these specific examples. For instance, the Regenerative Agriculture Alliance is a partnership of businesses and activists dedicated to furthering regenerative agriculture as a strategy for developing a more equitable and sustainable food system. Parallel to this, the Rodale Institute and a number of top organic businesses launched the Regenerative Organic Certification program, which attempts to provide a strict standard for regenerative agriculture and give customers a way to recognize and support such agricultural methods.

Regenerative agriculture is also being supported by the government through policies and programs. Farmers that embrace regenerative strategies like cover crops and no-till farming can receive financial aid and technical support from the USDA's Natural Resources Conservation Service (NRCS). Such initiatives are included in the Common Agricultural Policy of the European Union to support sustainable and regenerative agricultural methods.

Of course, there are also difficulties and barriers that prevent regenerative agriculture from being widely used. The predominance of conventional farming methods, the requirement for farmers to re-learn and adapt to new methods and approaches, and the dearth of financial incentives and support for regenerative practices are a few of these. There is cause for optimism about the future of this method of farming, too, as regenerative agriculture gains popularity and support, as well as rising acknowledgement of its advantages for farmers, consumers, and the environment.

Regenerative agriculture is a potent and exciting method of farming that has the ability to change our food system and heal the earth. Regenerative agriculture presents a sustainable and resilient road forward for agriculture by concentrating on repairing soil health, enhancing biodiversity, saving water, and reducing climate change. We have cause to be positive about the future of this significant movement given the rising awareness and support for regenerative agriculture, as well as the real-world examples and efforts that are now in place.

CHAPTER ELEVEN

Our food system could change thanks to regenerative agriculture, which also has the ability to tackle some of the most serious environmental and social issues of the day. However, a number of policy adjustments will need to be undertaken to encourage the broad adoption of regenerative techniques in order to fully fulfill this potential.

A key policy adjustment that is required is more funding for research and teaching. This covers financing for studies into the ecological and financial advantages of regenerative agriculture, as well as outreach and education initiatives to assist farmers in becoming familiar with and implementing regenerative practices. Many farmers want to switch to regenerative farming methods, but many lack the information and funding to do so. Policymakers can promote the shift to regenerative agriculture and make sure that farmers have the resources and knowledge they need to thrive by funding research and teaching.

The establishment of financial incentives for regenerative techniques is a crucial policy reform that is required. Due to financial limitations, such as the high cost of inputs like fertilizers and pesticides, many farmers are currently forced to stick to conventional agricultural methods. Policymakers can assist farmers in the transition to more sustainable and regenerative farming techniques by offering financial incentives for regenerative measures, such as tax breaks or subsidies. In addition to helping the environment and society at large, this will also help farmers financially in the long run by lowering input costs and raising agricultural yields.

In order to enable the widespread adoption of regenerative agriculture, regulatory adjustments will also be required. Changes to zoning laws, building codes, and other rules that make it challenging for farms to embrace regenerative practices may fall under this category. Because of zoning restrictions that are intended to shield residential areas from the odors and sounds associated with farming, many farmers are currently unable to raise cattle on their land. Policymakers can promote the shift to more sustainable and resilient agricultural systems by amending these regulations to permit for a wider variety of and regenerative farming practices.

There is a need for more cooperation and coordination between policymakers, farmers, and other stakeholders in addition to these policy improvements. This entails the creation of public-private partnerships and other cooperative projects that unite many stakeholders in order to work toward a common objective. Together, governments, farmers, and other interested parties can create more thorough and effective plans for advancing regenerative agriculture and solving the problems that our food system faces.

Regenerative agriculture is increasingly being recognized for its significance in tackling some of the most critical environmental and social issues of our time. However, considerable regulatory changes at the local, state, and federal levels will be required in order to fully realize the promise of this farming strategy. Policymakers may promote the shift to more resilient and regenerative agricultural systems by funding research and education, offering financial incentives, updating regulatory frameworks, and encouraging better cooperation and coordination.Regenerative Agriculture and Policy

CHAPTER TWELVE

Scaling up Regenerative Agriculture

Regenerative agriculture has enormous potential to revolutionize our food system and heal the planet. Yet, in order to attain its full potential, regenerative agriculture must be expanded to reach more farmers and consumers worldwide. This will necessitate a concerted effort on the part of governments, non-governmental organizations (NGOs), farmers, and consumers to invest in regenerative agriculture research, education, and policy, as well as to build markets that value regenerative methods.

Increased access to knowledge and training for farmers is a crucial strategy for scaling up regenerative agriculture. Many farmers may be unaware of regenerative approaches or lack the finances or support to put them in place. Farmers can implement regenerative practices and increase their productivity and profitability by providing access to knowledge, training, and technical assistance.

Another approach is to develop laws and programs that encourage and support regenerative agriculture. Governments can provide financial incentives to farmers that use regenerative approaches, as well as engage in regenerative research and education. They can also provide technical assistance and extension services to farmers in order to assist them in implementing regenerative practices.

Organizations and charitable groups can also help to scale up regenerative agriculture. These organizations can give money for new regenerative techniques and technology, as well as assistance with farmer education and training. They can also seek to create markets for regeneratively grown food by collaborating with shops, restaurants, and other purchasers to promote and sell regenerative products.

Consumers can help to accelerate the growth of regenerative agriculture. By purchasing regeneratively produced food, customers can assist to develop demand for regenerative techniques and markets for regenerative products. Consumer education and awareness initiatives can assist to spread the word about the benefits of regenerative agriculture and urge more people to support it.

Finally, to scale up regenerative agriculture on a worldwide scale, international cooperation and collaboration will be required. Several countries confront similar difficulties in terms of food security, environmental degradation, and social fairness, and regenerative agriculture offers a possible solution. Countries can collaborate to promote regenerative agriculture and establish a more sustainable and equitable food system for all by exchanging information, resources, and best practices.

To summarize, scaling up regenerative agriculture would necessitate a collaborative effort by governments, non-governmental organizations (NGOs), farmers, and consumers to invest in research, education, and policy, as well as to build markets that reward regenerative methods. We can fulfill the full potential of regenerative agriculture to alter our food system and heal the planet by improving access to knowledge and training, rewarding and supporting regenerative practices, developing markets for regenerative products, and partnering on a global scale.

CHAPTER THIRTEEN

Regenerating our Future

Regenerative agriculture has the ability to revolutionize our food system while also healing the environment. Regenerative agriculture, by focusing on concepts such as soil health, biodiversity promotion, and lowering dependency on synthetic inputs, offers a possible answer to many of the difficulties confronting our planet today, such as climate change, soil degradation, and biodiversity loss.

To fully fulfill the potential of regenerative agriculture, however, action at all levels of society, from individual consumers to governments and international organizations, is required. We will look at the important actions we can take to regenerate our future through regenerative agriculture in this chapter.

The first task is to raise awareness and educate people. Many people are still ignorant of regenerative agriculture's ability to address environmental concerns while also creating a more sustainable and equitable food system. We must raise public knowledge and understanding of the concepts of regenerative agriculture, as well as the benefits it provides for both people and the environment. Educational initiatives, public campaigns, and media outreach can all help.

The second phase is to provide assistance to farmers and groups who are already engaged in regenerative agriculture. These farmers are at the forefront of the fight to alter our food system, frequently working in the face of a variety of economic and social constraints. We can help them by purchasing food from regenerative farms, helping with farm organizations, and pushing for regenerative agriculture policies.

The third step is to allocate funds to research and development. While there is a growing corpus of research on the benefits of regenerative agriculture, much remains unknown about the most effective techniques and how to scale up regenerative agriculture to satisfy the demands of an expanding world population. We must invest in research to better understand the science of regenerative agriculture and to create new tools and technology to assist farmers in adopting regenerative methods.

The fourth phase is to develop incentives and policies to encourage regenerative agriculture. Governments and international organizations can play an important role in developing policies and programs that encourage regenerative agriculture, such as research and development funding, subsidies for farmers who use regenerative practices, and rules that promote soil health and biodiversity. We can help to level the playing field for regenerative farmers and encourage more farmers to adopt regenerative techniques by developing these incentives and policies.

The last phase is to lobby for structural change. Regenerative agriculture is about improving our entire food system, not simply changing farming practices. We must push for laws and practices that promote a more sustainable and equitable food system, such as those that encourage local food systems, limit food waste, and encourage fair labor practices. We must also address the underlying causes of environmental concerns, such as climate change and biodiversity loss, by campaigning for policies that reduce greenhouse gas emissions while also protecting biodiversity.

Finally, regenerative agriculture provides a tremendous solution to many of the issues confronting our globe today. Regenerative agriculture offers a viable path toward a more sustainable and equitable food system by focusing on principles such as improving soil health, boosting biodiversity, and lowering dependency on synthetic inputs. To fully fulfill the potential of regenerative agriculture, however, action at all levels of society, from individual consumers to governments and international organizations, is required. We can regenerate our future by working together to create a more just, sustainable, and resilient world.